Praise for Hell Fire Pepper Jelly

"Jenkins Jellies Hellfire Pepper Jelly…works for breakfast, lunch, dinner and dessert on a daily basis in my house. I particularly love it with some semi-soft pecorino smeared on warm crusty bread."
– MARIO BATALI, CHEF, RESTAURATEUR AND AUTHOR OF
Molto Batali: Simple Family Meals from My Home to Yours

"Forget a pinch of salt or spoonful of sugar. All you need is some Hell Fire! In your hands is a veritable treasure trove of deliciously easy and sinfully flavorful recipes, starring one of my favorite culinary finds. My advice: buy in bulk."
– DAPHNE OZ, CO-HOST OF TV'S THE CHEW

"Hooahhhh! (To) the ladies who manufacture the flamethrower jelly: More power to them! The military has a need for a new consumable form of napalm. That is a terrific product."
– GENERAL GEORGE PRICE

"Wake up your taste buds with Jenkins Jellies' Hell Fire Pepper Jelly. It doesn't taste like anything else you've ever had. Both sweet and hot, it'll become your new favorite condiment."
– TODAY'S DIET & NUTRITION MAGAZINE

"We love Hell Fire Pepper Jelly. Such a great flavor – sweet and hot, yet it holds the pepper flavor well! Cannot beat that combination! I see it as a glaze for seafood or just a small amuse bouche crostini with goat cheese and a small dollop of Hell Fire. Very nice!"
– CHEF Z. ZACKARY ZIAKAS, DIRECTOR OF SALES, FOR THE GOURMET

Cooking with Jenkins Jellies
HELL FIRE PEPPER JELLY

Happy Hell Fire!
Enjoy
Hillary Hanner
2013

Cooking with Jenkins Jellies
HELL FIRE PEPPER JELLY

Hillary Danner *and* Maria Newman

Foreword by GWYNETH PALTROW

Sweet Heat

ISBN-13: 978-0-9832726-6-3

Library of Congress Control Number: 2012941705
CIP information available upon request

First Edition, 2012

St. Lynn's Press . POB 18680 . Pittsburgh, PA 15236
412.466.0790 . www.stlynnspress.com

Book design–Holly Rosborough
Editor–Catherine Dees

Photo credits: Hillary and Maria author photo © 2012 Ed Gohlich Photography, Inc.
Photos on cover, pp. vi, 32, 49, 53, 70, 71 © Laurie Bailey. All other food
and product photos © Hillary Danner.

Copyrighted pepper photos on divider page spreads: Table of Contents: Pierre Selim;
Appetizers: Epp; Desserts: Mai Lei; More Sweet Heat Jellies: Forest & Kim Starr

Printed in The United States of America
on FSC recycled paper using vegetable-based inks.

This title and all of St. Lynn's Press books may be purchased
for educational, business, or sales promotional use.
For information please write:
Special Markets Department . St. Lynn's Press . POB 18680 . Pittsburgh, PA 15236

10 9 8 7 6 5 4 3 2 1

For Danner and Emma:
I love you to the moon and back,
infinity and beyond – infinity times.
I love you more.

HILLARY

⁓⚘⁓

For my loving and supportive family:
to Michael for his patience and encouragement
and to Rylee, my raison d'être.

MARIA

Table of Contents

RECIPES

Foreword

⟋⟍

*H*illary and I grew up mostly across the George Washington Bridge from each other – me in Manhattan, Hillary in Englewood, New Jersey. My mother and her father are siblings and very close. I cannot even begin to count the number of times our respective families traversed that bridge to spend time together as a family. The occasion? Meals. Christmas, Easter, a party, a random Sunday…meals were always what brought us together. That was the excuse; we just all wanted to be together. My mother and her father had come from a home where meals were festive and carefully prepared.

Our mutual grandmother was an amazing cook and entertainer and it absolutely trickled down to us. What a beautiful legacy to pass down: the love of good food, of cooking for friends and making an occasion out of it. Hillary and I always had this is common, and do to this day…cooking for people we love, eating, hanging out as a family. It's how we were raised. It's what we do.

On one of these occasions, not long ago, Hillary brought something special. It was in an unmarked jar of a sumptuous orangey color. It was something she and her friend Maria Newman had created and perfected. When I dipped a spoon into it and put it in my mouth, I swooned. Here was the most amazing, original, exploding flavor combination I had experienced in a long time… it was Hell Fire Pepper Jelly. It was at once sweet and savory, spicy and ambrosial, totally unique. I became obsessed. I had jars of it everywhere.

Hillary (on left) and me

I slathered it on sandwiches, mixed it into salad dressings, and used it on cheese boards. I haven't stopped yet.

When Hillary told me she and Maria were creating a cookbook based around this brilliant creation, my heart skipped a beat! In this fantastic collection of recipes, Hell Fire Pepper Jelly takes center stage with all its bursting excitement. Never again will I be stumped for new ways to use this magical ingredient. Raging Roasted Chicken? Fire and Ice Cream Sundae? Hell Fire Choco-tini? I'm trying them all. But I'm never giving up my Hell Fire Pepper Jelly on a fresh baguette with some sharp cheddar cheese – quite possibly my favorite breakfast ever.

Bon appétit!

Gwyneth Paltrow

Introduction

*W*e – Hillary and Maria – have been friends for over fifteen years. Several years ago we concocted a sweet and spicy jelly that had a profound effect on folks. After four years spent together in the jelly

trenches – learning the food-scene ropes, vending at local food festivals and indie craft fairs, as well as sharing some ol' fashioned blood, sweat and tears – we found ourselves in the middle of a real business. As the business continues to grow, Hell Fire Pepper Jelly keeps inspiring people to experiment with old recipes and really heat up the kitchen!

Now, we're writing a real cookbook, because people keep asking us: "How did you come up with this?"…"How else can I use it?"…"Ever think about doing a Hell Fire Pepper Jelly cookbook?" So here it is – *Sweet Heat* – a compilation of our favorite recipes along with recipes from chefs, passionate foodies and friends alike, who were excited to contribute their own Hell Fire discoveries!

HOW WE STARTED

Hillary's story

Hell Fire Pepper Jelly has its beginnings in the cozy backyard of my family home in Los Angeles. Filled with an abundance of fruit trees, this secret, urban garden became both a beautiful blessing and huge undertaking. I was at a crossroads after putting an acting career on hold to take care of a five-year-old son and infant daughter. I planted a vegetable garden nestled amongst the fruit trees, but soon the romance of all the fruit trees and veggies began to fizzle as I watched them rot and fall to the ground. Unable to consume all the edible treasures in time, I quickly taught myself how to can and preserve. After a while Maria got into the act, aiding and abetting my obsession, and soon Meyer lemon marmalades and apple plum butters were taking over my kitchen. While it was a fun, creative and rewarding experience, I still needed a job!

Maria's story

Growing up in Northern Canada, I eagerly awaited each summer because there was no snow, no school…and it was canning season, my favorite thing. I have fond memories of this yearly ritual, from picking out the produce at our local farmers market to inhaling the aroma of all that goodness simmering on the stove. Enjoying summer's bounty as fall and winter set in again was my delicious reward for all that hard work. As a grown-up now living in California, I wanted a reconnect with this wonderful tradition, so when my dear friend Hillary was starting to turn her preserving hobby into something more, I jumped on board. The rest is Hell Fire history.

Jenkins Jellies is born

When Hillary's mother-in-law suggested we try canning a jalapeño pepper jelly, neither of us had ever heard of such a thing. And, frankly, we thought it weird. Still, not knowing a bit about peppers or even liking spicy foods, we gave it a try and…gosh darn it, it was good! Hillary's Aunt Blythe took a few jars to her friend, actress Kate Capshaw (Mrs. Spielberg). That's when things really heated up! Kate loved the jelly and wrote to us saying that if we could spice it up and really make it our own unique thing, she would buy a case and send it to chef Mario Batali. Amazed, and thinking it a fun challenge, we started working on Hell Fire Pepper Jelly. With seven of the most beautiful peppers from Hillary's secret garden, some trial and error (and lots of hilarity and stinging eyes) – we got the balance down, bottled it up and took Hell Fire Pepper Jelly on the road!

And our name? "Jenkins" is a nickname bestowed upon Hillary. One day when she was stirring a pot of jelly on the stove, a friend came through the kitchen and exclaimed, "Jenkins! Making some jellies!" So Jenkins Jellies it became.

Someone else is born, too!

While we were joyfully up to our ears with our new company and new book, Maria found herself expecting a new addition to her family. So while *Sweet Heat* is a labor of love from the both of us, many of the recipes will be introduced by Hillary…because Maria has been deep in the throes of first-time motherhood. The Jenkins Jellies gang is happy to announce that Rylee Sofia Newman was born March 16th, 2012 – screaming for Hell Fire!

JOIN OUR FOODIE ADVENTURE

We had some serious fun gathering and testing the recipes in our book. We encourage you to play around with how others have incorporated our pepper jelly into these recipes, and we hope you'll make some of your own discoveries. Please share them with us (www.jenkinsjellies.com), because we have learned over and over again that the uses of Jenkins Jellies Hell Fire Pepper Jelly are endless and scrumptious! And remember... always ADJUST added jelly amounts to your preferred taste levels.

We hope you enjoy *Sweet Heat!*

Hillary & Maria
(and George, our
Jenkins Jellies mascot)

P.S. Just so you know – in the
recipes, we often use the
abbreviation "HFPJ" for
Hell Fire Pepper Jelly.

Appetizers

Melt-Me Baked Brie

Crostini with Avocado & Hell Fire

Doubly Deviled Eggs

Nuts on Fire!

Lox Mini Roll-ups

Cheese Wafers

Harry's Hummus & Pita Chips

Over-the-Top Cheese Plate / Stuffed Olives

Melt-Me Baked Brie

Dr. Bella Doshi

My father has been getting everyone on a Hell Fire kick — he even gifted a jar to his dentist, Bella Doshi, who served it the following way at a family Christmas gathering. She presented it with water crackers and exclaimed afterwards, "It was a BIG HIT!"

YOU WILL NEED:

1 (8-oz.) wheel brie cheese
Hell Fire Pepper Jelly, to taste
½ of a 17-oz. package frozen puff pastry

WHAT TO DO:

Preheat oven to 350 °F.

Slice the wheel of brie in half horizontally — Dr. Doshi used dental floss, of course.

Spread HFPJ in the middle of the bottom half and place the other half on top. If you wish, spread a little more jelly on the top half.

Wrap the whole wheel of brie in the puff pastry and bake 15-20 minutes. Let cool 5 minutes before serving.

Serve with crackers or sliced baguette.

Crostini with Avocado & Hell Fire

Pastry Chef Laci Kjellsen

This amazing treat came from Laci Kjellsen, whom we met while presenting our Hell Fire at the San Francisco Gift Show. She tasted our jelly and immediately suggested this recipe from her favorite vegan bar, Encuentro. Boy, are we glad she did – this appetizer is one of our favorites!

MAKES ABOUT 30 CROSTINI

YOU WILL NEED:

1 French baguette
Fresh garlic
Olive oil for brushing and drizzling (regular or garlic flavored)
3–5 ripe avocados
1 jar Hell Fire Pepper Jelly *
Sea salt (black sea salt is fun for added color, but any sea salt will do –
   we used grey sea salt in this photo)
Fresh cilantro for garnish

WHAT TO DO:

Preheat oven to 375°F.

Slice baguette thinly, biscotti-style.   Rub fresh garlic on top of each slice, then brush with olive oil.

Arrange prepared bread slices on a cookie/baking sheet and toast in the oven (middle to upper rack) for about 10 minutes, or until just lightly browned.

Remove from the oven and place on a platter for assembling: Place thick slabs of avocado atop each bread slice. Spoon HFPJ (gingerly!) over the avocado, and drizzle with more olive oil.

Shake sea salt over layered crostini and top with a sprig or two of fresh cilantro.

For another dimension, add shaved or crumbled bits of cheese – like Manchego or pecorino.

* If your guests crave more heat, keep the jar of HFPJ on the table, along with a spoon.

Doubly Deviled Eggs

Katharine Danner

My grandmother taught me how to set the stage – to entertain – and how to always make my guests feel welcomed and special. One of her signature appetizers was her deviled eggs. They are still the best I've ever tasted. Mixed with a little Hell Fire… they are out of this world!

MAKES 12 DEVILED EGGS HALVES

YOU WILL NEED:

6 hard boiled eggs
2 tablespoons mayonnaise
1½ tablespoons Hell Fire Pepper Jelly
2½ tablespoons sweet relish
Paprika, for sprinkling

WHAT TO DO:

Shell hard boiled eggs (a bit easier to do under running water), and slice in half lengthwise.

Scoop out yolks and place in a mixing bowl with the rest of the ingredients (except the paprika). Mix well and adjust to taste.

Evenly fill the white part of the eggs with the yolk mixture.

For a little more zest, place a small dollop of Hell Fire Pepper Jelly on each egg and lightly sprinkle with paprika.

Sure to be a Hell Fire hit!

Nuts on Fire!

Chef Jared Levy

Jared used pecans here, but you can get adventurous and throw in some almonds, walnuts or peanuts. These candied lovelies can be stored for up to two weeks. Keep them covered at room temperature. Adding desiccant packets or oxygen absorbers will keep the nuts fresher, longer.

MAKES 1 QUART (4 CUPS) CANDIED NUTS

SPECIAL TOOLS NEEDED

Candy thermometer
Non-reactive saucepan (i.e., stainless steel or non-stick. NO ALUMINUM)

YOU WILL NEED:

2 cups Hell Fire Pepper Jelly
1 cup water
4 cups pecan halves
1½ quarts canola oil

WHAT TO DO:

In a saucepan, combine HFPJ and water over low heat. Heat until consistency resembles maple syrup (about 5 minutes).

Add nuts to syrup, stirring gently, until nuts are coated. Keep stirring until slightly tacky, then remove nuts and cool on a cookie sheet or grated cooling rack.

Heat oil in a non-reactive saucepan. Using a candy thermometer, bring oil to 310°F.

Fry cooled nuts in small batches (½ cup at a time). This is important for maintaining the oil's temperature. Fry each batch of nuts for about 2 minutes. The nuts are ready when they rise to the surface and the oil stops fizzing or bubbling. Remove nuts from pan with a slotted spoon and allow to cool on the cooling rack.

Lox Mini Roll-ups

Danner Renfro

My son, Danner, LOVES salmon and he suggested I include a sushi roll in our cookbook. This seemed way beyond my ability – so we compromised and came up with this easy appetizer. The ingredient amounts are up to you. Pile on as much cream cheese, Hell Fire Pepper Jelly and salmon slices as you like. This is a great DIY dish for an informal party.

MAKES 6 MINI ROLL-UPS PER TORTILLA

YOU WILL NEED:

Flour tortillas
Cream cheese
Hell Fire Pepper jelly
Smoked salmon, sliced

WHAT TO DO:

Lay a tortilla flat and spread a layer of cream cheese on top.

Spread desired amount of HFPJ over the cream cheese.

Finally, layer the salmon slices and roll the tortilla.

Cut into 6 pieces and serve.

Did You Know?
The powerful capsaicin (kap-sa-ə-sən) found in chilies is used to make pepper spray.

Cheese Wafers

Aimee Basa

Ron Basil, one of our first Hell Fire die-hard fans (and a great friend of my father's), shared our pepper jelly with his daughter, Aimee – who in turn shared the following recipe with us. These cheese wafers are a cross between a wafer and a biscuit. We found them to be quite tasty paired with a dark, hearty stout or ale.

MAKES ABOUT 80 WAFERS

YOU WILL NEED:

2 cups flour
1 tablespoon sugar
¼ teaspoon salt
¼ teaspoon
   curry powder,
   optional
Pinch ground
   pepper
½ cup cold butter,
   cut up
8 oz. sharp
   cheddar cheese,
   shredded
3 tablespoons
   water
3 tablespoons Hell
   Fire Pepper Jelly
   (adjust to taste)

WHAT TO DO:

Pulse all ingredients in food processor until mixture resembles peas.

Gather dough into a ball and divide in half.

Shape each half into a 10" log. Wrap each log in plastic wrap and refrigerate for 2-24 hours.

Heat oven to 400°F and grease 2 cookie sheets.

Slice each log into ¼" slices and bake 8-10 minutes.

Cool on wire rack.

Note: You can reheat in 350°F oven and serve with an extra whollop dollop of Hell Fire.

Harry's Hummus & Pita Chips

Harry Danner

For years, my dad's famous hummus and pita chips has been requested at various parties and gatherings. Not wanting to mess with perfection, he was hesitant to mix it with the Hell Fire. BUT…now that he has, he says he'll never make it the old way again!

MAKES ABOUT 2 CUPS HUMMUS AND 72 PITA CHIPS

YOU WILL NEED:

1 (15-oz.) can organic garbanzo beans (chickpeas), rinsed and drained
3 heaping tablespoons sesame tahini (we recommend Joyva brand –
   and not to confuse this ingredient with tahini sauce)
3 medium-to-large cloves garlic
Juice of ½ lemon
¼ cup extra virgin olive oil
2½ tablespoons Hell Fire Pepper Jelly
Salt, to taste, optional

1 (12-oz.) package whole wheat pita bread (6 pita pockets)
Paprika, to taste

WHAT TO DO:

Preheat oven to 275°F.

Place garbanzo beans, tahini, garlic, lemon, olive oil, and HFPJ in a blender and blend until smooth. Add salt, if needed.

To make pita chips: Cut each whole pita into 6 wedges, then carefully separate the 2 layers of each wedge.

Arrange wedges on baking pans and heat in oven until golden brown, about 5-7 minutes. Don't burn!

Transfer hummus to a bowl, introduce a dollop of Hell Fire into the center, sprinkle lightly with paprika, and serve with your very own pita chips.

Over-the-Top Cheese Plate

The most universal (and arguably the easiest) way to enjoy your Hell Fire Pepper Jelly is with some cheese and a salted cracker. The first time we ever heard about pepper jelly, someone explained what you do with it: You get a slab of cream cheese, pour the jelly over it and surround it with Wheat Thins. That was just the start for us. We like to mix HFPJ with goat cheese, melt it with brie, smear it on aged cheddar – any good cheese. Pairing it with a salted cracker is key. Two of our favorites are: Trader Joe's Pita Crackers with Sea Salt, and Milton's Sea Salt Crackers. You can easily create a taste sensation that's sure to impress your spicier guests. And don't forget the olives!

Hell Fire Stuffed Olives

Serve these babies on the side of your cheese platter...or garnish a martini!

Spoon a little Hell Fire Pepper Jelly into pitted martini olives (if they are already stuffed with pimentos, just remove them with the tip of a sharp knife or fork). Spoon a little HFPJ into the olives and there you have it!

Sauces & Dips

QUICK & EASY HELL FIRE SAUCES

CREAMY DREAMY DIP

BAR BAR'S SALAD DRESSING

COOL-AS-A-CUCUMBER SAUCE

SPIRITED SAFFRON SAUCE

DEVIL'S OWN SATAY PEANUT SAUCE

VIETNAMESE-STYLE HFPJ SAUCE

Quick & Easy Hell Fire Sauces

Hillary Danner and Maria Newman

The easiest way to add some excitement to an ordinary dish is by mixing some HFPJ with your regular condiments. The possibilities are endless, but we're offering a few to get you started.

BASIC RECIPE FOR 1 CUP OF SAUCE:

½ cup condiment
½ cup HFPJ

WHAT TO DO:

Mix and enjoy.

Note: Our recipe is a 1:1 ratio, but hey it's your sauce, so experiment with a small amount until it's right for your taste buds…or your guests'!

Catsup and HFPJ: Use on hamburgers, hot dogs, meatloaf, French fries, eggs, etc.

Mustard and HFPJ (especially good with country-style Dijon): Use on sandwiches, hot dogs, salad dressings…whatever.

Mayo and HFPJ: Good with tuna salad, grilled cheese sandwiches, deviled eggs – anyplace you use mayo.

BBQ sauce and HFPJ: This goes wherever you use BBQ sauce: chicken, ribs hot wings, salmon, BBQ chicken pizza, just for starters.

Honey and HFPJ: Use in any dish where "hot and sweet" could use some extra "sweet."

Butter and HFPJ: Limited only by your imagination! Popcorn, definitely… but we even use it to baste our roasted peaches (see p. 86.)

Relish and HFPJ: Put some zing into your burgers, tuna salad and hot dogs.

Pesto and HFPJ: This is a whole new flavor high! We used it in the turkey panini recipe on p. 60.

Creamy Dreamy Dip

Susanne Young

This crudité dip comes from the kitchen of Susanne Young, the wife of my son's Cub Scout leader. She and her husband, Doug, have fed and put up with us Den 15 folks for the better part of 4 years of scouting and camping... and living. Their kitchen table and welcoming home have been important staples in our lives. Thank you!

MAKES 1½ CUPS

YOU WILL NEED:

½ cup cream cheese
1 cup sour cream
2 teaspoons Hell Fire Pepper Jelly
(as always, adjust to your liking)

WHAT TO DO:

Mix it all up in a bowl and serve with assorted veggies of your choice... or potato chips!

Bar Bar's Salad Dressing

Chef Barbara Beck

My mom and Barbara were big time Broadway dancers in the 60's – they were out shopping the day my mom went into labor with me! Barbara picked us up at the hospital and took us home in her VW Bug. I still, to this day, call them Bar Bar cars.

MAKES 1 CUP

YOU WILL NEED:

2 cloves garlic
2 teaspoons Dijon mustard
2 teaspoons garam masala (optional and available in ethnic food sections)
4 tablespoons balsamic vinegar
3 tablespoons Hell Fire Pepper Jelly, or to taste
4 tablespoons mayonnaise
4 tablespoons extra virgin olive oil

WHAT TO DO:

Place first six ingredients in a food processor and mix until smooth.

With the machine running, slowly add olive oil until blended.

Serve on a fresh, leafy salad!

Cool-as-a-Cucumber Sauce

Chef Norm Phenix

This refreshing combination makes an excellent sauce for grilled chicken.

MAKES 1 CUP AND A BIT MORE

YOU WILL NEED:

1 cup organic plain yogurt
2 tablespoons Hell Fire Pepper Jelly
1 cucumber, peeled and seeded
10 mint leaves

WHAT TO DO:

Place all ingredients in a food processor and blend until smooth.

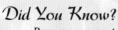

Did You Know?

Peppers are part of the fruit family and not vegetables. They're low in calories and packed with vitamin A to keep your eyes nice and healthy!

Spirited Saffron Sauce

Chef Barbara Beck

This lovely sauce goes with Barbara's "Tilapia with Panko Crust" on page 76. It is a natural with seafood dishes.

MAKES 1¼ CUPS

YOU WILL NEED:

For the sauce reduction:
1 cup white wine
¼ cup wine vinegar
¼ cup cider vinegar
3 sprigs fresh thyme
Generous pinch of saffron
3 tablespoons Hell Fire Pepper Jelly

Other ingredients:
½ cup mayonnaise (you can use Hell Fire mayo from
   p. 20, if you're brave)
½ cup sour cream

WHAT TO DO:

Bring sauce reduction ingredients to a low boil, and continue cooking until liquid is reduced to ¾ cup. Strain and let cool.

To complete the sauce: In a separate bowl, blend 6-8 tablespoons of the reduction with the mayonnaise and sour cream.

The remaining sauce can be saved in an airtight container in the fridge for 3 to 5 days.

28

Did You Know?

Cooking changes the heat in peppers: fresh peppers lose some of their heat when cooked, but dried peppers get hotter. So beware!

Devil's Own Satay Peanut Sauce

Chef Norm Phenix

Norm is co-owner of 204 Main Bar & Bistro in Sharon Springs, N.Y. We are thrilled that he incorporated our Hell Fire in this peanut sauce that he serves at the restaurant. It's really fantastic!

Norm says: "This wonderful sauce can be used in a variety of dishes. Serve it with beef or chicken satay or as a dip for crudités. It is also great in place of mayonnaise for a Thai chicken salad – just add scallions and julienned carrots, and serve over greens."

MAKES 1½ CUPS

YOU WILL NEED:

6 tablespoons smooth peanut butter
¼ cup Hell Fire Pepper Jelly
¼ cup soy sauce
2 tablespoons canola oil
¼ cup fresh lime juice (Key lime, if you have it)
1 tablespoon fish sauce (found in the ethnic section of your grocery store)
2 tablespoons freshly grated ginger
½ teaspoon cayenne pepper
3 teaspoons minced garlic
1 tablespoon sesame oil
2 tablespoons water

WHAT TO DO:

Combine all ingredients in a food processor and pulse together 6-8 times, or until mixture is smooth. After each pulse, scrape down sides to further incorporate into mixture. Transfer to a bowl.

31

Vietnamese-Style HFPJ Sauce

Chef Jared Levy

This version of a traditional Vietnamese sauce is called for in Jared's "Noodles From Hell" recipe on page 48. He suggests making it in advance, as the flavor will develop over the first three days. Can be refrigerated for up to one week.

MAKES ABOUT 1 CUP

YOU WILL NEED:

6 oz. Hell Fire Pepper Jelly
 (½ medium-sized jar)
3 garlic cloves, peeled and
 finely grated
2 tablespoons fish sauce
 (found in the ethnic section
 of your grocery store)
Juice of 2 limes
2 tablespoons water

WHAT TO DO:

Combine all ingredients and whisk until smooth.

Sides & Salads

ROASTED CORN WITH HELL FIRE BUTTER DRIZZLE

HARRY'S CORN SALAD

COLE SLAW FOR THE SOUL

ROASTED BRUSSELS SPROUTS

BAKED SWEET (HEAT) POTATOES

JAMMIN' YAMS

NOODLES FROM HELL

TWICE BAKED STUFFED POTATOES

MS. KAREN'S KICKIN' KORNBREAD

DOING CORN, HARRY DANNER'S WAY

Roasted Corn with Hell Fire Butter Drizzle

Growing up in my house, cooking corn was some serious business! I was always a bit nervous while awaiting the corn outcome and my father's satisfaction with its "doneness." No smushy corn kernels allowed! Yes indeed, there was a certain "crunch" that he aspired to – and now so do I. So I figured my "kernel king" dad was the one I should wrangle to experiment with roasting some Hell Fire corn.

There are so many ways to cook corn and so many ways to use it with the Hell Fire. Here are a couple of ideas to inspire you!

SERVES 4…OR 2, IF THE CORN IS THAT GOOD!

YOU WILL NEED:

4 ears of corn, with husks on
2 tablespoons melted butter
2-4 tablespoons Hell Fire Pepper Jelly, depending on desired heat
Salt and pepper, to taste

WHAT TO DO:

Prepare outdoor grill: Get those coals a burnin'.

Cut off one or both ends of the corn. Peel back and tear off one section of the cornhusks.

Soak corncobs in a pot of water for about 5 minutes, then place cobs on the grill to roast for about 30 minutes, turning them occasionally.

Meanwhile, prepare the Hell Fire Butter drizzle.

For the Hell Fire Butter: Melt butter and HFPJ together on the stovetop (or in a microwave for about 20 seconds).

Keeping the corncobs on the grill, baste exposed kernels with the butter mixture. Then remove from the grill and peel the remainder of the husks.

For a more consistent "roasted look" (and an opportunity for a final basting) put the cobs back on the grill for another minute or so and add more of the Hell Fire butter mixture. Or, just smother straight Hell Fire Pepper Jelly onto the cob!

Harry's Corn Salad

Harry Danner

MAKES 3 CUPS

YOU WILL NEED:

4 ears of corn, cooked (you can use from the Roasted Corn recipe if you like,
  or prepare on the stovetop)
1 tablespoon butter, melted
2 teaspoons Hell Fire Pepper Jelly, adjust to taste
¼ cup diced purple onion
1 cup cherry or plum tomatoes, cut in half
Salt and pepper, to taste

WHAT TO DO:

Slice the cooked kernels off the cobs and place in a mixing bowl. Melt
butter and HFPJ together and pour over corn. Mix in the onion and
tomatoes. Season with salt and pepper to taste…and of course some more
Hell Fire, too – if you dare!

Did You Know?

*Parrots and other tropical birds LOVE snacking on hot peppers. But
don't kiss your little friend on the beak or you'll have burning lips!*

Cole Slaw for the Soul

Hillary Danner

I planted some purple cabbage in my garden this year, in hopes of using it for this recipe…didn't happen. With the clock ticking on the cookbook deadline, I bee-lined to Fresco's Market and picked up a bag of the pre-shredded stuff — fast, easy and delicious! Can't wait to try it fresh from the garden.

MAKES 6 SMALL SIDE SERVINGS

YOU WILL NEED:

14-oz. package shredded cabbage/carrot mix
1½ cups mayo/Hell Fire mix (1:1 ratio of mayo to HF sauce – see page 20)
Juice of ½ lemon (regular or Meyer)
Salt and pepper, to taste

WHAT TO DO:

Mix all the ingredients in a bowl. Grind a little extra pepper on top and serve.

Did You Know?

Chili peppers are addicting! Endorphins, our body's natural painkillers, are released to combat the capsaicin-induced heat factor. This creates a feeling of wellbeing… and then we want more!

Roasted Brussels Sprouts

Catherine Cutright

While premiering our jellies at the San Francisco International Gift Show, we stayed at our friend Catherine's home. When we presented her with a jar of our jelly for the first time, she raced to the refrigerator, found some Brussels sprouts and went to work. We were amazed.

SERVES 2 TO 3

YOU WILL NEED:

1 lb. Brussels sprouts (about 16 sprouts)
3 tablespoons extra virgin olive oil (or try a roasted garlic-infused one, too!)
3 tablespoons Hell Fire Pepper Jelly
1 teaspoon kosher salt

WHAT TO DO:

Preheat oven to 375 °F.

Cut off and discard ends of Brussels sprouts, then cut them in half lengthwise. Rinse in cold water and drain.

Place sprouts on a baking sheet or baking pan. Coat sprouts with olive oil and HFPJ, and sprinkle with salt. Mix together with your hands until sprouts are coated evenly.

Place in the oven and cook for 15-20 minutes. Halfway through the cooking time, quickly toss or mix the sprouts around the pan so they roast evenly.

Don't overcook. You don't want them to get mushy!

43

Baked Sweet (Heat) Potatoes

Diane Behrens

Our friend Diane is a super talented painter and actress. She has been a BIG Hell Fire fan from the start…and she's the daughter of cookbook author Helen Kindler Behrens ("Diplomatic Dining"). We thought Diane's take on Hell Fire was a must!

MAKES 4 HALVES

YOU WILL NEED:

2 whole sweet potatoes
4-6 tablespoons butter, divided
8 tablespoons sour cream
8 tablespoons Hell Fire Pepper Jelly, divided
½ cup chopped pecans or walnuts
¼ cup brown sugar, optional
Salt and pepper, to taste

WHAT TO DO:

Preheat oven 425°F.

Wash, scrub and dry sweet potatoes. Rub the outsides with butter and place on a baking sheet

Bake for 40 minutes to 1 hour, depending on size of potatoes. Halfway through baking time, poke with a fork to allow some steam to escape.

Meanwhile, in a small bowl, mix together sour cream and 6 tablespoons of HFPJ.

When potatoes are finished baking, remove from oven and slice in half, lengthwise (careful not to burn yourself!). Break up the insides a bit and slather each half with remaining butter and HFPJ, letting it seep into the

crannies. If you wish, now is the time to add that brown sugar, salt and/or pepper!

Dollop the sour cream mixture over each half and sprinkle with the chopped nuts. Oh, yeah!

Jammin' Yams

Chef Jared Levy

Jared and Hillary were childhood pals, growing up in Englewood, NJ. Lucky for us that he became such a talented chef! A note from Jared: "Vegetables seem to really absorb the Hell Fire heat, so keep that in mind when preparing this dish. This side dish is a true sweet heat treat!"

SERVES 6

YOU WILL NEED:

4 yams, peeled and cubed
2 green apples, cored and cubed
½ cup Hell Fire Pepper Jelly
¼ – ½ cup brown sugar or maple syrup

WHAT TO DO:

Preheat oven 375°F.

Combine all ingredients in a bowl and mix well.

Transfer to a baking dish and cook for 40 minutes, or until done, stirring once or twice during cooking.

Did You Know?

How do you know how hot a pepper is? In general, the smaller, the hotter. All the world's hottest peppers are less than three inches long.

Noodles from Hell

Chef Jared Levy

This recipe was inspired by Jared's time studying cooking in Vietnam. The sauce is based on his friend and fellow chef Viet Tham's mother's recipe – a staple found in most Vietnamese homes. It's delicious! This version is made with shrimp, but you can substitute tofu.

Note: *The recipe for Vietnamese-Style HFPJ Sauce is on page 32. It can be prepared ahead.*

SERVES 4 TO 6

YOU WILL NEED:

1 package cold cellophane rice noodles
½ lb. deveined shrimp
Salt and pepper, to taste
1 tablespoon olive oil
1 cup Vietnamese-Style HFPJ Sauce (see note above)
1 carrot, shredded or finely julienned
1 Persian cucumber, shredded or finely julienned
1 scallion or green onion, finely chopped
1 jalapeño, sliced into rings
3 sprigs cilantro
1 sprig mint
1 sprig Thai basil

WHAT TO DO:

Prepare cold rice noodles according to instructions on package. Set aside.

Rinse, pat dry and lightly salt and pepper the shrimp. Cook seasoned shrimp over high heat in a pan with olive oil, about 1-2 minutes on each side. Set aside.

In a large mixing bowl, combine noodles, shrimp, Vietnamese-Style HFPJ Sauce, and all remaining ingredients (except the cilantro, mint, and Thai basil). Toss together and let marinate for 20 minutes.

Just before serving, sprinkle with fresh herbs, toss again and SERVE!

Twice Baked Stuffed Potatoes

Hillary Danner

I have to admit I had never made a baked potato before this attempt. The mashed version has always been my favorite, so I went to my grandmother's 1953 and 1964 versions of The Joy of Cooking to have the proper schooling in how to bake a potato. My first lesson learned: Don't wrap the potatoes in aluminum foil! After making this recipe, I shared the results with my neighbors, who texted me back with, "Those were the best taters we've ever had!"

MAKES 4 POTATO HALVES

YOU WILL NEED:

2 whole baking potatoes
2-4 tablespoons butter, divided
3 tablespoons sour cream
2 tablespoons Hell Fire Pepper Jelly
½ teaspoon salt
¼ cup Manchego cheese (grated)
¼ cup sharp cheddar cheese (grated)

WHAT TO DO:

Preheat oven to 425°F.

Wash, scrub, and dry potatoes.

Rub the outsides of each with about ½ tablespoon of butter.

Place on a baking sheet and bake for 40 minutes to 1 hour (more or less, depending on size).

About halfway through baking time, take potatoes from oven and poke small holes with a fork to allow steam to escape. Return potatoes to oven.

Once cooked, remove potatoes from oven and slice each in half lengthwise.

Preheat broiler.

Scoop out potato insides (careful not to damage skins) and place in a medium-sized bowl.

In a smaller bowl, mix sour cream and HFPJ. Add sour cream/jelly mixture, salt, and remainder of butter to bowl with potato insides. Mash and mix well, then spoon mashed potato mixture evenly back into the 4 half-potato skins.

Sprinkle tops with Manchego and cheddar cheese.

Broil potatoes for about 5 minutes, or until cheese is melted and edges are slightly golden brown. Be aware: Broiling happens quickly, so watch that they don't burn!

Ms. Karen's Kickin' Kornbread

Karen Hayes

This brilliant idea came from my daughter's ballet teacher, Karen Hayes—who is not only quite the twinkle-toed dance teacher, but also a foodie! When she got her hands on our Hell Fire Pepper Jelly, she thought…cornbread!

If you have a favorite cornbread recipe use it; otherwise, our pick is Trader Joe's Cornbread Mix, which can be prepared with optional vegan ingredients.

MAKES 9 SERVINGS (USING TRADER JOE'S CORNBREAD MIX)

YOU WILL NEED:

1 box Trader Joe's cornbread mix (15 oz.)

For the mix, you will need:
1 egg (or a vegan substitute: 1 banana)
½ cup oil
¾ cup milk (or a vegan substitute, like rice milk)

Additional ingredients:
⅓ cup Hell Fire Pepper Jelly
½ cup Manchego cheese, optional but delicious!

WHAT TO DO:

Preheat oven to 350°F.

In a large mixing bowl, beat together egg, oil and milk (or vegan equivalents for egg and milk). Stir in cornbread mix until just moistened.

Add the HFPJ and cheese. Mix a little more.

Pour batter into greased 8x8x2 pan and bake until golden brown, about 35-40 minutes. To test for doneness, insert a knife in the center until it comes out clean.

If you want a little more spice: brush some extra HFPJ atop the finished cornbread.

Main Dishes

CURRIED TOFU TEMPTATION

CHINESE HELL FIRE SHRIMP

POWERFUL PESTO TURKEY PANINI

PIZZA STU WITH PIZZAZZ

WHITE HOT BIANCA PIZZA

PHILLY CHEESE FAJITA SANDWICHES

PANINI CAPRESE

RAGING ROASTED CHICKEN WITH VEGETABLES

SHRIMP WITH COCONUT MILK & SOBA NOODLES

GRAVLAX (CURED LOX) WITH HFPJ

TILAPIA WITH PANKO CRUST AND SPIRITED SAFFRON SAUCE

Curried Tofu Temptation

Linda Miller

I'm a bit of a novice when it comes to doing anything with tofu. It either completely falls apart for me or it's tasteless. Well, this suggestion from my lovely neighbor Linda Miller has changed the tofu game for me!

SERVES 4

YOU WILL NEED:

1-2 tablespoons olive oil, enough to coat the pan
1 (14-oz.) package organic firm tofu, sliced about ¼" thick
½ cup Hell Fire Pepper Jelly
½ cup yellow curry sauce (we used Thai Kitchen's 10-minute Simmer Sauce)
¼ cup fresh basil, sliced thinly

Prepared rice of your choice

WHAT TO DO:

Coat a frying pan with olive oil and heat on medium. Arrange tofu slices in the pan and lightly fry both sides for about 6-10 minutes, total time.

Meanwhile, combine the HFPJ and yellow curry sauce in a bowl and whisk well.

Pour sauce over the tofu, lower the flame and let simmer for 10 minutes. Halfway through the simmering, toss in fresh basil.

Serve over a bed of rice.

57

Chinese Hell Fire Shrimp

Jason Renfro

This recipe was inspired from a dish Jason and I enjoyed for years at the Mandarette Chinese Café in Los Angeles. This one really showcases the spice in the Hell Fire Pepper Jelly – so be sure to adjust accordingly.

SERVES 4

YOU WILL NEED:

½ cup panko bread crumbs
2 teaspoons sea salt, coarse
2 cups or 20 shrimp (1 lb.), shelled, deveined and no tails
6 tablespoons mayonnaise, divided
½ cup peanut oil, plus 1 tablespoon extra for sauce
1 tablespoon minced garlic
3-5 tablespoons Hell Fire Pepper Jelly
1 cup shelled walnuts, roughly chopped

2 cups prepared rice
¼ cup diced bell pepper, preferably a colorful variety
4 scallions, thinly sliced

WHAT TO DO:

Mix panko, salt, shrimp and 2 tablespoons of mayonnaise in a zip bag. Shake to mix well.

Heat peanut oil in a skillet with minced garlic. As garlic starts to lightly brown, lower to medium heat and add shrimp. Cook shrimp until done, about 6 minutes per side. Remove shrimp and place on plate with paper towel to drain off some oil.

In a clean pan over medium-low heat, combine HFPJ, 4 tablespoons mayonnaise, and 1 tablespoon oil. Mix until uniform in color. Stir in walnuts.

Just as sauce begins to bubble, add shrimp. Continue stirring and let simmer for 1-3 minutes.

Serve over prepared rice and sprinkle with the raw bell peppers and scallions.

Powerful Pesto Turkey Panini

Hillary Danner and Maria Newman

We LOVE a good Panini here at Jenkins Jellies. A favorite of ours is this turkey panini. We encourage you to change it up however you see fit – but this is how we like it best!

MAKES 1 PANINI

YOU WILL NEED:

1 ciabatta rustic roll
2 tablespoons extra virgin olive oil, divided
Salt and pepper, to taste
Hell Fire Pesto Sauce (1:1 ratio of pesto to Hell Fire Pepper Jelly; see p. 21)
Mayonnaise, to taste
2 turkey slices
2 tomato slices
3 fresh buffalo mozzarella slices

WHAT TO DO:

Slice the roll in half and drizzle with olive oil. Sprinkle salt and pepper, if desired. Generously spread the Hell Fire Pesto Sauce on one half of the roll and the mayonnaise on the other half. Layer the turkey, tomato and cheese and close the sandwich.

If you have a panini maker, use it! If not, just heat a pan on the stove, coat with olive oil and place the assembled sandwich in the pan. Flame should be medium to medium-low so the panini gets warmed all the way through, but does not burn.

Flip the panini over a few times, putting some sort of weight (a cast iron pan?) on the sandwich to get the smushed panini effect. Or just push down

with a metal spatula. It will be tasty no matter how you cook it, or what it looks like.

Serve with Hell Fire Pesto Sauce on the side, because you will want to spread some more on while devouring your panini!

Pizza Stu with Pizzazz

Titina Folliero

Titina Folliero is the owner of Folliero's Pizza, an establishment that her father started over 40 years ago. It's a staple in Highland Park, California's food scene. Not only is the pizza delicious, but our kids (and moms) are also great buddies, and we find ourselves eating there a bunch. One day I brought in a jar of Hell Fire Pepper Jelly and we went to town!

MAKES ONE 12-INCH PIZZA

Note: Prepare pizza dough or purchase pre-made pizza dough prior to beginning recipe.

YOU WILL NEED:

Prepared pizza dough for one 12-inch pizza, plus flour for rolling out
1-2 tablespoons Hell Fire Pepper Jelly
½ cup prepared tomato/ pizza sauce
1 tablespoon grated Parmesan cheese
1 large tomato, sliced (or use a few of the Roma variety)
1 4-6-oz. fresh mozzarella ball, sliced
2 cups fresh arugula

WHAT TO DO:

Preheat oven to 400°F.

Roll out prepared pizza dough on a lightly floured surface.

Spoon pepper jelly onto the dough and spread evenly. Add a layer of tomato sauce, spreading it gently over the jelly. Place the sliced tomato over the sauce and sprinkle with Parmesan cheese.

Place pizza on a pizza stone or baking sheet and bake for about 15 minutes.

Remove from oven and arrange slices of mozzarella on top of pizza. Return to oven for another 5 minutes. Pizza edges should be lightly golden and mozzarella need not be completely melted.

Remove pizza when done and generously top with fresh arugula!

White Hot Bianca Pizza

Titina Folliero

Folliero's Bianca was the one that inspired us to try our Hell Fire on a pizza. Without a tomato-base sauce to complicate the flavors, Hell Fire became the star of the show!

MAKES ONE 12-INCH PIZZA

Note: Prepare pizza dough or purchase pre-made pizza dough prior to beginning recipe.

YOU WILL NEED:

Prepared pizza dough for one 12-inch pizza, plus flour for rolling out
1-2 tablespoons Hell Fire Pepper Jelly
3 cloves fresh garlic, thinly sliced
Fresh rosemary, to taste, about 1 teaspoon
1 cup shredded mozzarella
Extra virgin olive oil, just a drizzle

WHAT TO DO:

Preheat oven to 400°F.

Roll out prepared pizza dough on a lightly floured surface.

Spoon HFPJ onto the dough and spread evenly. Layer the sliced garlic over the jelly. Then sprinkle

with fresh rosemary (remember, rosemary has a very strong taste, so adjust to your liking!). Evenly disperse the cheese over the pizza.

Place pizza on a pizza stone or baking sheet and bake for about 20 minutes, or until pizza edges are lightly golden and cheese is bubbling.

Remove from oven, drizzle olive oil over the finished pizza and serve!

Philly Cheese Fajita Sandwiches
William Boyd

We are so appreciative of Fresco Community Market, as they have welcomed our jellies with open arms! This special grocery store is devoted to bringing awareness and support to the local community. One of their team members, William, excitedly shared this recipe with us – and we are so glad he did!

This recipe can produce four variations: beef, pork, chicken, or vegetable fajita, pre-marinated from the grocery store. Pick one or try them all!

MAKES FOUR 5-INCH-LONG SANDWICHES

YOU WILL NEED:

2, 10-inch bread loaves (hoagie style)
4-6 tablespoons olive oil, divided
1 tablespoon (more or less) crushed garlic
Salt, a couple of pinches, or to taste
¼ lb. marinated fajita (either beef, pork, chicken or veggie)
2 bell peppers (yellow and red, sliced lengthwise)
2 portabella mushroom caps (about 6 oz.) sliced
1 red onion
4 slices Swiss cheese
Hell Fire Pepper Jelly, to taste

WHAT TO DO:

Slice bread loaves in half, lengthwise. Drizzle (or brush on) olive oil to insides of sliced bread. Spread garlic over olive oil and sprinkle with salt.

Grill bread, oil side down, on stovetop – or toast in oven. Set aside.

Pour olive oil in a saucepan and sauté your fajita of choice on the stovetop. As fajita mixture is cooking, add HFPJ and continue to sauté until meat is cooked through. Set aside.

In a separate saucepan, heat and sauté olive oil, peppers, onions and mushrooms until tender. Add extra HFPJ to mixture, if desired.

Once peppers, onions and mushrooms are cooked through, separate them into piles and place a slice of cheese over each. Let melt.

To assemble sandwiches: Spread desired layer of HFPJ on toasted bread. Place cooked fajita mixture on bread, then layer with a sautéed pile of peppers, onions, mushrooms and cheese.

Serve open-faced or closed (you might need a toothpick to secure a closed sandwich).

To make more than one type of fajita sandwich at a time, sauté mixtures together in a larger pan or separately.

Panini Caprese

Take any favorite panini or sandwich to a new level with our Hell Fire Pepper Jelly. Here's a simple example to start. Add or subtract as you see fit.

MAKES 1 PANINI

YOU WILL NEED:

1 ciabatta roll
1 tablespoon Hell Fire Pepper Jelly
4 slices fresh mozzarella
4 slices Roma tomato
2 large leaves fresh basil
1 tablespoon extra virgin olive oil
Salt and pepper, to taste

WHAT TO DO:

Slice the roll in half, horizontally, and pull out some of the dough from both halves.

Spread the HFPJ on both halves and layer the mozzarella, tomato slices and basil.

Drizzle olive oil all over, and salt and pepper.

Enjoy as is (or grill it in a pan for another dimension of goodness).

Did You Know?
The longer chilies are allowed to mature on the vine the hotter they become.

Raging Roasted Chicken With Vegetables

Chef Jared Levy

Chef Jared says, "This recipe calls for roasting the chicken and vegetables together, but keep in mind that during cooking the vegetables will tend to absorb more of HFPJ's heat, while the spicy aspect of the chicken may diminish. Here's an option: If you want to up the ante on the chicken's spice factor without overpowering the veggies, you could roast the vegetables and the chicken separately."

SERVES 4

YOU WILL NEED:

3½ lb. chicken
3 teaspoons kosher salt, divided
1½ teaspoons black pepper, divided
1 head garlic, intact and unpeeled
   (cut top off to release flavor)
1 lemon, quartered
1 sprig rosemary
3 carrots, peeled and roughly
   chopped (about ¾ inch)
1 lb. fingerling potatoes, halved
1 lb. pearl onions, peeled
1 tablespoon thyme, de-stemmed and
   finely chopped
8 tablespoons Hell Fire Pepper Jelly,
   divided
2 tablespoons hot water

WHAT TO DO:

Preheat oven to 375°F.

Rinse chicken and pat dry. Liberally salt and pepper the inside of the bird, then stuff with the whole head of garlic, lemon and rosemary.

In a mixing bowl, combine vegetables, thyme, 2 teaspoons salt, 1 teaspoon black pepper and about 4 tablespoons HFPJ. Toss until coated.

Coat roasting pan with olive oil. Layer the bed of the pan with vegetables and set the chicken on top.

Combine 4 tablespoons HFPJ with 2 tablespoons hot water. Using a pastry brush, coat the chicken with the jelly/water mixture.

Salt and pepper the outside of the chicken.

Place the pan in the oven and cook for 45 minutes to 1 hour, or until the internal temperature of the chicken reaches 165°F. Baste every 15 minutes with more pepper jelly and rotate vegetables.

Active basting during cooking will make for an extra tasty bird with a nice crispy, almost caramelized, skin.

Shrimp with Coconut Milk and Soba Noodles

Chef Barbara Beck

From Broadway dancer to clothing designer to chef/owner of her own catering company in New York City – Barbara lends us some of her kitchen wizardry and love for the taste of Thai in this recipe.

SERVES 4 AS A MAIN COURSE OR 6 AS A FIRST COURSE

YOU WILL NEED:

1 tablespoon finely chopped garlic
1 tablespoon finely chopped fresh ginger
2 jalapeños, finely chopped
6 scallions, cut into ¼-inch diagonal slices
2 tablespoons extra virgin olive oil or canola oil
1 (13.5 oz.) can coconut milk, divided (not "Light")
2-3 tablespoons Hell Fire Pepper Jelly, or to taste
1 tablespoon Wondra flour
1 lb. or 21-25 shrimp (peeled, deveined and tails off)
⅓ small bunch fresh coriander, chopped with stems
Salt, to taste

Soba noodles, green or other (2 bundles of an 18 oz. 4-bundle package, or ½ package other soba noodles (about ½ lb.)

WHAT TO DO:

Sauté garlic, ginger, jalapeños and scallions in oil over medium heat for about 2 minutes. Add ½ the coconut milk and the HFPJ, and simmer for a few minutes to dissolve and blend flavors. Salt to taste.

Mix remainder of coconut milk with the flour and stir into sauté mixture for slight thickening.

Add shrimp and cook until almost done, then add coriander and remove pan from heat. Let sit until noodles are ready. Note: You can prepare shrimp mixture a couple of hours ahead and reheat.

For the noodles: Bring water to a boil in a large 4-quart pot. Add noodles and cook for about 3 minutes or until done. Drain and add to shrimp mixture. Or dish individual portions of noodles and top with shrimp mixture.

Gravlax (Cured Salmon) with HFPJ

Chef Jared Levy

Never heard of gravlax? Gravlax comes from Scandinavian words for salmon and grave – meaning "buried salmon." In the Middle Ages, fishermen preserved salmon by salting it and burying it in the sand to cure. Jared shares his super-easy way to cure salmon. It will keep in the refrigerator for one week after curing. Try it with bagels and cream cheese, onions and capers…the classic combo.

Or try it as an appetizer, and make the Lox Mini Roll-Ups on page 10.

MAKES 1 POUND OF GRAVLAX

YOU WILL NEED:

1 lb. filet of a good piece of salmon
1 cup Hell Fire Pepper Jelly
1 cup salt

WHAT TO DO:

Place salmon in a non-reactive container (glass, food grade plastic or stainless steel) and set aside.

In a small mixing bowl combine salt and HFPJ and spread the mixture over all sides of the salmon.

Seal container and refrigerate for 4-5 days, or until salmon is no longer soft to the touch. EACH DAY: Check salmon and redistribute any of the salt/jelly mixture that might have dropped off.

After 4-5 days, when curing is complete, rinse the salmon filet and pat dry.

Slice thinly and serve.

Note: You can use the same recipe to cure your own bacon. The result is not spicy, just delicious.

Tilapia with Panko Crust and Spirited Saffron Sauce

Chef Barbara Beck

Barbara enjoys cooking with spices, leaning towards Thai and Indian flavors, which she feels go perfectly with our Hell Fire in the sauce that accompanies this taste-pleasing tilapia dish.

SERVES 4-6

Note: The saffron sauce should be prepared ahead (recipe on page 28).

YOU WILL NEED:

4 tilapia filets
2 tablespoons flour
1 extra large egg, beaten
1½ cup panko crumbs (Japanese breadcrumbs found in most markets)
2 tablespoons olive oil for frying
1 cup Spirited Saffron Sauce (see note above)

WHAT TO DO:

Slice each filet down the center. You now have 8 pieces.

Dust the top side of each with flour. Dip floured side into the beaten egg, then press lightly into panko crumbs, to create an even layer for the crust. Set aside or refrigerate until ready to cook.

In a large frying pan over medium heat, fry filets in oil, crumb side down, until dark golden brown. Turn the filets and fry on medium-low for about 2 more minutes.

To serve: Top each piece of fish with 2 tablespoons of Spirited Saffron Sauce, or place sauce in a side dish for dipping.

If you're preparing the fish ahead: Don't completely cook the second side; instead, cook the second side for only one minute and remove from heat. Then reheat in the oven at 375°F until warm, or reheat on top of the stove.

Desserts & Treats

PEANUT BUTTER & HELL FIRE COOKIES

DARING DONUT HOLES

ROASTED DONUT PEACHES WITH ICE CREAM

PEPPER JELLY S'MORES

FIRE & ICE CREAM SUNDAE

Peanut Butter & Hell Fire Cookies

Hillary Danner

This peanut butter cookie was my granddad's favorite. My "mutti," Katharine Danner, made it for him all the time. It's an unexpected twist on a classic. We often sample this combo at food events, where one very happy sampler exclaimed, "It's like a spicy nutter-butter!" We agree.

MAKES 36 SMALL COOKIE "SANDWICHES"

YOU WILL NEED:

½ cup shortening (Crisco or similar)
½ teaspoon baking soda
¼ teaspoon salt
½ cup peanut butter
½ cup granulated sugar
½ cup brown sugar
1 egg, well beaten
1 cup flour
Hell Fire Pepper Jelly
Whole shelled peanuts, 1 per cookie

WHAT TO DO:

Preheat oven to 325°F.

In a large bowl, beat shortening until light. Add baking soda, salt and peanut butter and beat well together. Gradually add the sugars, creaming well, then add beaten egg and finally the flour.

Roll into small balls (about ½-teaspoon-size of dough per ball) and place on ungreased cookie sheet. With a fork, press each cookie 2 times, making a criss-cross pattern.

For half of the cookies: Place a dab of HFPJ on top, and a peanut. Leave the rest of the cookies without jelly or peanut – those will become the bottom layer of the cookie sandwiches.

Bake for 18–20 minutes. Do not overcook. Remove baked cookies and assemble tops and bottoms, with a helping of jelly in between.

A sweet and spicy treat!

Daring Donut Holes

Chef Jared Levy

Jared put his own twist on this recipe, which was inspired by Chef Jordan Toft at the trendy Eveleigh Restaurant in L.A. We served up these delectable goodies at a couple of L.A. food events and they proved to be an extremely popular and unexpected treat!

MAKES ABOUT 2 DOZEN

Note: The dough needs to be refrigerated overnight and you will need a pastry bag and piping tip.

YOU WILL NEED:

8 eggs (room temperature)
1 (¼-oz) package yeast
⅓ cup sugar
3⅓ cups bread flour
1 teaspoon powdered nutmeg
1 tablespoon salt
1 lb. butter, cubed

4 cups oil, for frying
½ jar, or 6 oz. Hell Fire Pepper Jelly (for piping a dollop into each donut hole)

WHAT TO DO:

Bring eggs to room temperature and whisk together in a bowl.

Add yeast and place into mixer with paddle attachment in place. Add sugar, flour and nutmeg, and mix together for 10 minutes. Add salt and butter cubes and mix until butter is smooth and well incorporated.

Transfer dough mix to a separate bowl, cover with plastic wrap and let sit in the refrigerator—**overnight**.

TO MAKE THE DONUT HOLES:

On a floured surface, roll out a portion of the dough to about $1/3$-inch thick.

Cut out 1-inch diameter circles and place onto a well-floured tray. Allow dough to rise to $2/3$ inch (double in size).

Heat oil in pot to 350°F. Deep-fry donuts in small batches until golden brown. Let dry on paper towels.

Pipe in HFPJ (while donuts are still warm), using a pastry bag and tip.

Serving options:

Roll donuts in powdered sugar or a mixture of cinnamon and sugar, and serve.

Drizzle some (as pictured) ChocoBoost on the donut holes and serve.

Do all of the above and knock the socks off your guests... OH, YES!

Roasted Donut Peaches with Ice Cream

Hillary Danner and Maria Newman
(with thanks to the Fresco Community Market team)

While we were sampling our jellies at Fresco Community Market, one of their team members introduced us to the adorably scrumptious donut peaches. He suggested we grill them with our Hell Fire Pepper Jelly – and so we promptly did! Scrumptious indeed!

SERVES 4

YOU WILL NEED:

4 ripe donut peaches
Hell Fire butter mixture
    (1-2 tablespoons HFPJ
    and 1-2 tablespoons
    melted butter)
4 scoops vanilla ice cream
Fresh mint to garnish

WHAT TO DO:

Place whole donut peaches on prepared grill and cook for a couple of minutes. Then flip over and grill a few minutes more.

Prepare the Hell Fire butter mixture: Melt butter and HFPJ together on the stovetop (or microwave for about 20 seconds).

Flip peaches one more time, so the bottoms are touching the grill. Brush tops with butter mixture and watch for the peaches to start to bubble on top. Brush with more butter mixture. Cook for another 8 minutes or so, letting them get nice and juicy and warm.

Remove roasted peaches and put in 4 serving bowls with a scoop of ice cream. Garnish with a sprig of mint and drizzle some more Hell Fire butter over the whole thing!

Pepper Jelly S'mores

Pastry Chef Laci Kjellsen

Laci is pastry chef at San Francisco's Taste Catering. Laci says: "Here at Taste we make our s'mores completely from scratch! And they're round! We make our own graham crackers, marshmallows and chocolate ganache squares. I'm including our graham cracker dough recipe here, but you can simplify by using purchased graham crackers."

MAKES 12 MINI S'MORE SANDWICHES

YOU WILL NEED:

1 bar Hershey's Dark Chocolate
6 standard-sized marshmallows
24 Graham Cracker O's from Graham Cracker Dough
   recipe below (or 24 store-bought graham crackers)
¼ cup Hell Fire Pepper Jelly

GRAHAM CRACKER DOUGH

1 cup butter (soft, room temp)
¾ cup brown sugar, packed
3 tablespoons honey (room temp)
1½ cups all-purpose flour
1 cup graham flour or whole wheat flour
½ teaspoon salt
1 teaspoon baking soda
1 teaspoon cinnamon

WHAT TO DO:

For the homemade graham crackers *(if using store-bought grahams, skip to the assembly steps)*

Preheat oven to 350°F.

In an electric mixing bowl with paddle attachment, cream together butter and brown sugar until soft and fluffy. Drizzle in honey.

Sift all dry ingredients together and add to mixture.

Once dough is mixed completely, turn it out onto a flat, lightly floured surface. Gently roll dough out to about 1/8" thick. Slide it onto the back of a baking sheet or onto a cutting board, and place in refrigerator to chill for at least one hour, covered lightly.

Remove dough from refrigerator and punch out your first graham cracker "O", slightly larger than the diameter of a marshmallow end. Punch out the rest of the dough until you have 24 O's. (Option: Sprinkle the tops with cinnamon and sugar before baking to make them extra special.)

Arrange graham cracker shapes on a flat baking sheet lined with parchment paper and bake for about 10 minutes, or until brown around edges. Remove from oven and place O's on a work surface.

To Assemble S'mores: Reduce oven temp to 300°F.

Cut marshmallows in half width-wise with a sharp knife, creating two short, round disks.

Break the chocolate into pieces no larger than the width of a marshmallow.

Choose the flattest graham O's (or square grahams, if store-bought) to be the bottom halves of s'mores and flip them over so top of the cookie is lying flat on counter top.

Dab a small amount of pepper jelly onto the grahams and place marshmallows on top of jelly. Toast marshmallows with a kitchen torch until lightly brown (see note 1, below). Dab another bit of pepper jelly onto the marshmallows and top with the chocolate and second graham.

Place s'more stacks onto the parchment-lined baking sheet and warm in oven until chocolate is slightly melted. This helps them stick together. Yum!

Notes: If you do not have a kitchen torch you can use a skewer and roast the marshmallow over a gas stove burner – the same way you would at a campfire!

Bob's Red Mill offers a great graham flour and can be found in most health food stores.

Substitute one cup of pork lard for one cup of butter to add a rich and delicious flavor!

Fire & Ice Cream Sundae

Karen Klemens

Karen is a fellow jammer, who holds a degree as a Master Preserver. She incorporates her homemade jellies and preserves into the organic ice cream she makes and offers at her wonderful establishment, Mother Moo Creamery in Sierra Madre, CA. We incorporated her Szechuan Pepper and Salty Chocolate ice creams with the Hell Fire for this spectacular treat!

MAKES 1 SUNDAE

YOU WILL NEED:

Two scoops of your favorite ice cream flavors
1–2 tablespoons Hell Fire Pepper Jelly, or to taste
1–2 tablespoons chocolate sauce, or to taste
¼ cup candied nuts, roughly chopped (see our "Nuts On Fire!" recipe
    on page 8)

WHAT TO DO:

Scoop the ice cream into a dish. Spoon the jelly directly from the jar onto the ice cream in a zigzag pattern. Drizzle with chocolate sauce and sprinkle candied nuts on top.

Devour!

Drinks

Hot Hot Cocoa

Maria Newman

Hell Fire Pepper Jelly goes sooooo well with chocolate. We thought we'd try something wacky and throw it in our hot cocoa. For extra oomph, we also mixed some HFPJ in the whipped cream!

MAKES 1 CUP

YOU WILL NEED:

Your favorite hot cocoa mix
1 teaspoon Hell Fire Pepper Jelly (adjust to your liking)
Whipped cream (optional)

WHAT TO DO:

Follow directions for your hot cocoa and add the Hell Fire Pepper Jelly, starting with a small amount until you've got the perfect flavor blend for your taste buds. Top with a dollop of whipped cream, if you like.

That's it!

Did You Know?

Is your mouth on fire? Forget the water or ice cubes and grab some milk or a spoonful of yogurt! The reason? Capsaicin. It's the oil in the chilies that brings out the heat in the hot. And as we know, oil and water don't mix.

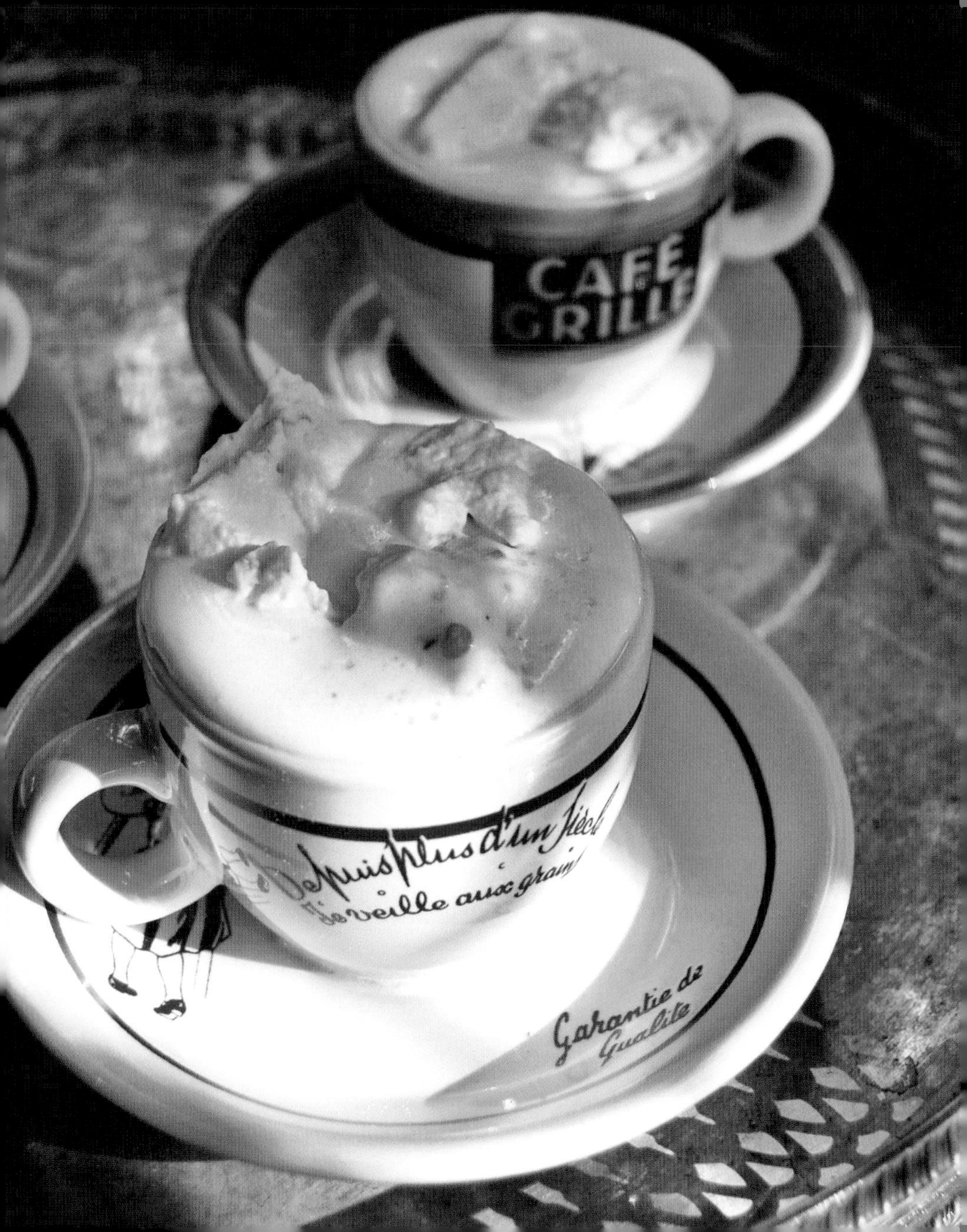
Garantie de
Qualité

Strawberry Chili Chill Smoothie

Chef Norm Phenix

What's not to like about this energizing smoothie! Plug in your blender, 'cause things are about to perk up. A perfect summer cool-down with a subtle kick.

MAKES 1 SMOOTHIE

YOU WILL NEED:

1 cup organic plain yogurt
1 tablespoon Hell Fire Pepper Jelly
1 cup sliced ripe strawberries
10 mint leaves

WHAT TO DO:

Place all ingredients in a food processor and blend until smooth.

On an entirely different note: A variation on this recipe, substituting cucumber for strawberries, makes an excellent sauce for grilled chicken. See Norm's "Cool-as-a-Cucumber Sauce" on page 26.

Did You Know?

The Trinidad Scorpion Butch T pepper is officially the world's hottest chili pepper. On the Scoville scale (that measures pepper heat) it measures 1,463,700. A bell pepper measures 0, and a jalapeño is a mere 3500-8000.

Mixed Drinks
Laura Ann Masura

"There's a whole lot of shaking going on," says Laura Ann, "but that's what you need to really break up and incorporate jam/jelly flavors into cocktails. It is a chilling technique but also introduces much-needed air into juice- and jam-based drinks. I always use a Boston shaker, but whatever shaker you use, make sure to REALLY shake these up to get the most of the sweetness and pepper taste in your Hell Fire drinks." Laura Ann is an artisan preserve maker, mixologist and nice lady from Laura Ann's Jams…and General Manager of El Cid restaurant in Los Angeles.

Dangerous Daiquiri

This is the classic daiquiri. But many people think of "daiquiri" as a frosty, frozen drink… so you could also toss this bad girl into a blender with a little ice and serve as a frozen drink.

YOU WILL NEED:

3 oz. light rum (Laura Ann uses Bacardi Light)

1-oz. spoonful Hell Fire Pepper Jelly

¾ oz. fresh lime juice

WHAT TO DO:

Shake well. Strain into cocktail glass.

Tantalizing Choco-Tini

For a great sugar rim: Chill your glass. Mix some sugar with a dash of cocoa powder and a tiny bit of cayenne pepper. Wipe the rim with an orange slice and dip the glass in the spicy sugar mix.

YOU WILL NEED:

1 oz. Godiva liqueur

3 oz. Stoli orange vodka

1-oz. spoonful Hell Fire Pepper Jelly

WHAT TO DO:

Shake well. Strain into spicy cocoa-rimmed glass.

Garnish with a little pepper or maybe even a little orange slice!

Or...you could get crazy and garnish with whipped cream and sprinkle the choco/spicy/sugar on top of the cream. Take that cocktail straight to dessert!

A Kicking Mule

(the Hell Fire version of a Moscow Mule)

Without a doubt THE favorite at El Cid's bar. A classic Moscow Mule has a spicy ginger kick, but the Hell Fire Pepper Jelly takes it to new, spicy heights! People are always surprised and keep coming back for more.

YOU WILL NEED:

2 oz. vodka
1 oz. lime juice
Dash of bitters
1-oz. spoonful Hell
  Fire Pepper Jelly

WHAT TO DO:

Shake well. Pour over ice in a Collins glass.

Add 4–5 oz. ginger beer. Garnish with a lime wedge.

Some-Like-It-Hot Lime Rickey

(You COULD add booze, but a lime Rickey is usually a non-alcoholic cocktail.)

YOU WILL NEED:

4 oz. lime juice
1-oz. spoonful Hell Fire
    Pepper Jelly
3 dashes of bitters

WHAT TO DO:

Shake well. Pour over ice in a Collins glass

Add soda water to fill glass. Garnish with lime peel.

More Sweet Heat Jellies

GUAVA BRAVA
(HAWAIIAN HOTTIE GUAVA PIZZA)

FIERY FIGS
(ENCHILADA WITH FIERY FIGS MOLE SAUCE)

PASSION FIRE
(PASSION FIRE POPCORN)

Hawaiian Hottie Guava Pizza

Titina Folliero

Guava Brava is one of our newest jellies. Just like our other jellies, it got its start from the bountiful trees in our "secret garden." For our Hawaiian Hottie pizza we started with Titina's basic pizza recipe, then gave it a tropical-spice zing with Guava Brava. After tasting it, we say, "Brava, guava!"

MAKES ONE 12-INCH PIZZA

Note: Prepare pizza dough or purchase pre-made pizza dough ahead.

YOU WILL NEED:

Prepared pizza dough for one 12-inch pizza, plus flour for rolling out
1–2 tablespoons Guava Brava Jelly (or Hell Fire Pepper Jelly)
½ cup prepared tomato/pizza sauce
1 cup shredded mozzarella
¾ cup pineapple, bite-sized chunks
½ cup ham, sliced thinly

WHAT TO DO:

Preheat oven to 400 °F.

Roll out prepared pizza dough on a lightly floured surface.

Spoon jelly onto the dough and spread evenly. Layer the tomato sauce and lightly spread evenly over the jelly. Sprinkle with mozzarella cheese. Add the pineapple and ham.

Place pizza on a pizza stone or baking sheet and bake for about 20 minutes, or until pizza edges are lightly golden and cheese is bubbling.

Remove from oven when done and serve!

Enchilada with Fiery Figs Mole Sauce

Linda Miller

I am blessed to have Linda as my neighbor for several reasons: She is kind and generous, babysits my dogs on a whim, and is quite the cook. There is a little shelf built within the fence that divides our properties. We meet there often to exchange a piece of wrongly delivered mail, a cup of sugar or the puppies for a play date. One day I looked out and the following fixings were perched on the ledge (I'm glad I got it before our rooster did!) This classic enchilada recipe gets its sweet heat on with a Fiery Figs mole sauce.

MAKES 6 ENCHILADAS

YOU WILL NEED:

1 whole chicken breast
Salt and pepper, to taste
2 tablespoons olive oil (add more as needed for frying)
1 small white onion, chopped (used either raw or sautéed)
6 tortillas (Linda recommends a ½ flour/ ½ corn version from Trader Joe's)
½ of a 28-oz. can of Las Palmas Red Chile Sauce
6-8 tablespoons Fiery Figs Pepper Jelly (adjust to taste)
1½ cups jalapeño jack cheese, shredded and divided

WHAT TO DO:

Preheat oven to 350°F

Lightly pound chicken breast, then season with salt and pepper.

In a pan with oil, quickly fry the tortillas. Remove each from pan and set aside.

Using the same oiled pan, sauté the chicken with the onions until cooked.

Place the cooked chicken on a cutting board and slice, chop or cube it. Then place the chicken, onions and 1 cup cheese in a bowl, and mix it all up.

To make the mole sauce: In a separate bowl, mix together the Red Chile Sauce and the Fiery Figs Pepper Jelly.

Dip each tortilla in the mole sauce. Then place them on a lightly oiled baking dish, spread the chicken mixture on top, roll it all up, drizzle on some more Fiery Figs mole sauce to cover (you may add more water to the sauce if you need a bit more); and sprinkle the top with the remaining ½ cup cheese.

Bake for 10 minutes.

Serve with a side of sour cream or avocado – whatever sounds good to you!

Note: Linda prefers not to bake her enchiladas, but makes them individually and zaps them in the microwave for about 45 seconds. Both ways turn out beautifully.

Passion Fire Popcorn

Bonnie Shugrue

Bonnie is my very first friend in the world; 14 months older, she visited me in the hospital the day I was born. Now she's a busy mother of three and has recently ventured back to teaching full-time. After one crazy week with school and family, she was far too exhausted to make anything but popcorn and she spiced it up with a bit of our Passion Fire Pepper Jelly! Now we have taken Bonnie's simple idea a couple steps further. Check it out!

MAKES 4 QUARTS POPPED CORN

YOU WILL NEED:

⅔ cup yellow popcorn
6 tablespoons cooking oil
¼ cup butter
¼ cup Passion Fire Pepper Jelly
Salt, to taste

WHAT TO DO:

Heat cooking oil and one kernel of popcorn in a large, heavy, covered pan. After kernel pops, pour in rest of popcorn. There should be enough kernels to cover bottom of pan but no more than one kernel deep.

Cover and shake until all corn is popped.

Melt butter and Passion Fire Pepper Jelly together on the stovetop (or in a microwave for about 20 seconds). Mix well and pour over the hot popcorn.

Sprinkle some salt, if you wish, toss and voilà!

Note: The recipe calls for cooking popcorn on the stovetop, but you will get the same results with microwavable popcorn.

Acknowledgments

In our quest to pepper the world with Hell Fire Pepper Jelly, we have been blessed with an inordinate amount of support and encouragement. We've found that conquering one tastebud at a time is hard work! Our army of angels and foot soldiers have carried us through many a dark moment and we are forever grateful to you all!!! Thanks for every hand lent and all the words of wisdom.

It takes a village.

Unique LA founder Sonja Rasula, for your astounding devotion to the local artists; we are forever grateful for the stages you set for us all to grow (stateofunique.com). Fresco Community Market owners Jon Murga and Helena Jubany, for welcoming us with open arms, and to Robert Chavez for being a super cool guy (frescomarkets.com).

Kristoffer Winters, for insisting the jelly business was the way to go! Pauline Parry, owner of Good Gracious Events, for opening her kitchen to us as we transitioned from home hobby to something bigger. To Jared and Viet, for kicking Harry and Hillary out of Pauline's kitchen and showing us how to get from 40 jars to 400 in a day!

Artisanal LA founder Shawna Dawson, for your encouragement and support from the very beginning. Mike McMurtry for all those Milton's Sea Salt crackers that taste so good with our jelly!

Debra Prinzing, for getting the ball rolling on this book (debraprinzing.com). Laila Villalobos, for always having our back, and Laurie Bailey for your beautiful photos (lauriebailey.com). Big kudos to our website guru Lorelei McCollough (customwebsitedesignservices.com), Kelli Ivie, Lauren Taplinger, Bella McGuan, our intern Aidan McCollough, Da'Kine Foods, Staci Trexler, Jennifer Asher, Penny Vizcarra, and our friends at The Highland Park Heritage Trust.

Karen Klemens of mothermoo.com, Chris Vamos of milkmanla.com; www.chocoboost.me; and Chef Alessandra of orgasmodelaboca.com: your artisanal products are stupendous! Jack Surran: thanks for showing Hillary her way around a camera so she could do justice to the recipes... and to Laurie Bailey (lauriebailey.com), for adding your beautiful food photos to our book. Susan Woods of Crier PR, for kindly introducing us to the game. Special thanks to Mario Batali and Kate Capshaw.

To Gwyneth, of course – for changing our jelly-game by announcing us to the world on GOOP! We are so grateful for your generous support and beautiful foreword.

To those generous, creative people who contributed their super-yummy recipes: Diane Behrens, Aimee Basa, Barbara Beck, William Boyd, Catherine Cutright, Harry Danner, Katharine Danner, Bella Doshi, Titina Folliero, Laci Kjellsen, Jared Levy, Laura Ann Masura, Linda Miller, Norm Phenix, Danner Renfro, Jason Renfro, Bonnie Shugrue, Susanne Young. Thank you!

Paul Kelly of St. Lynn's Press, for giving us this incredible opportunity; and Cathy Dees, for your gentle but firm lead on how to cross the finish line! And Holly Rosborough: thank you for your artistic encouragement. We needed it.

Roderick Smith is the artist extraordinaire! Your kindness and light truly inspire us. Since we all know it's really about the packaging, it's safe to say, without your beautiful labels we would be lost (rodericksmith.com).

Blythe Danner and Bruce Paltrow: we are eternally grateful. Harry and Dorothy Danner, for taking the biggest risk of all and making each day possible.

And finally, to George the rooster. They say roosters bring good luck. This one found us, and 4:45 a.m. will never be the same.

About the Authors

*H*illary Danner and Maria Newman live with their respective families in Southern California (Hillary hails from New York and Maria from Sudbury in Ontario, Canada). As friends and business partners for many years, their focus and passion is on eco-aware projects that benefit their community. With Jenkins Jellies, they are pouring their considerable energies into bringing unique artisanal condiments to a wide audience of adventuresome food lovers.

Find out more at
www.jenkinsjellies.com

A percentage of the profits from Jenkins Jellies is donated to the Bruce Paltrow Oral Cancer Fund (http://oralcancerfoundation.org/people/bruce_paltrow.htm) and to Green Wish (www.greenwish.com).